How to Crochet a Granny Square for Beginners

A Crochet Basics Tutorial

DEDICATION

D1607898

Contents

What Is a Granny Square?

You've likely seen granny squares before!

A granny square is a basic piece of square, crocheted fabric. Surprisingly, it is created by working in rounds from the center outward, rather than in rows. It usually has a lace-like appearance, with fairly large gaps between the stitches.

This type of project was first termed a granny square because it was made with a series of three double crochet stitches in the same space, referred to as granny clusters. However, the definition has since loosened, and granny squares can be structured in a wide range of ways—with or without granny clusters.

1

Basic granny square patterns are ideal projects for beginners because they are quick to make and use a small amount of yarn. However, they're not *only* for beginners; crocheters of all skill levels make granny squares because they can be used to assemble more complex projects, like blankets and sweaters.

What Are Granny Squares Used For?

On its own, a single granny square may not seem like a functional piece of fabric. However, crocheters typically make several granny squares, which they assemble together into blankets, scarves, sweaters, purses, and other larger projects.

Making granny squares is also commonly used for "stashbusting"— that is, using up all the leftover yarn odds and ends from previous projects, rather than letting it go to waste.

What Do You Need to Learn How to Crochet a Granny Square?

To learn to crochet granny squares, you just need a few basic supplies—which, if you've already started crocheting, you may already have.

Crochet hooks: To crochet, you need a single hook (unlike knitting, which requires two needles). To select the right size hook, check the label on your yarn for a recommendation—or try purchasing a variety pack of hooks, so you can easily try out a few different sizes.

Yarn: If you've ever been to the yarn aisle of a craft store, you know that yarn is available in a wide variety of colors, weights, and textures. For a granny square, try a worsted yarn, which is medium weight and perfect for most beginner patterns.

Stitch markers: Stitch markers can be useful to track locations in your granny squares, like the start of each round. This can help ensure your project ends up as a neat square, rather than slanted or circular.

Pattern: Especially if you're new to the craft, it's helpful to base your project on a pattern. Fortunately, there are plenty of free, easy granny square patterns for beginners.

New to Crochet? Tips, Tools, and Techniques

Modern Crochet: Essential Skills for Getting Started

Take the Class

Granny Square Crochet Patterns

Not all granny squares are the same. You can find granny square patterns that range from simple to complex (we're talking flower- and cat-themed granny squares!). As a beginner, aim to find an easy granny square crochet pattern that involves just one or two types of basic stitches. As you get more comfortable, you can move on to more complex pieces.

If you're ready to learn how to crochet a granny square, here are a few basic granny square patterns to get you started.

Easy Granny Squares for Beginners

A basic granny square can be created in just three rounds, using a few types of foundational stitches: chain, double crochet, and slip stitch.

Use this tri-color granny square pattern to create a traditional square using granny clusters, which are made up of three double crochets each. The pattern is easy enough for beginners, but it also gives you the option to incorporate three different colors (and explains the technique for switching yarn colors mid-square), so you can give your creations some variety. For a slightly larger square, try this pattern, which also involves a color change.

If you'd rather start with a single-color project, this classic granny square pattern is perfect. Once you understand the basic, repeating stitch pattern, you can complete the square very quickly—or, you can continue the pattern outward to create a larger square.

Solid Granny Squares

A solid granny square doesn't mean that it's created with a single, solid color—although you can certainly make it that way! Rather, a solid granny square doesn't have the gaps that you see in a more traditional, lace-like square.

True to its name, this solid granny square pattern has absolutely no gaps. The step-by-step tutorial explains how to successfully avoid the spaces that you would usually see in a granny square (hint: it has to do with eliminating the chain spaces and using triple crochet stitches to turn the corners).

This solid granny square pattern *does* feature a few small gaps in each corner, but that is a stylistic preference—the holes simply add character.

Single Crochet Granny Squares

Because traditional granny squares look like lace, they're not suitable for containing items—in other words, they're not ideal for making things like purses or pencil cases. However, single crochet granny squares, similar to solid granny squares, don't have gaps or holes. More specifically, however, single crochet granny squares are created using single rather than double crochets.

With this pattern, you can create a square with virtually no gaps—so solid, in fact, that it can be used to create a small box! The tutorial also provides some helpful tips in case your square starts curling or takes on a more circular shape, rather than a square.

Double Crochet Granny Squares

As you may have guessed from its name, a double crochet granny square is one that is made with double crochet stitches. In a pattern, you will see this type of stitch abbreviated as "dc." At first glance, these are very similar to single crochet or solid granny squares, but if you look closely, you will see that the double crochet stitch is taller than a single crochet stitch, giving the square a slightly different look.

In this pattern, double crochet stitches come together to form a fairly solid granny square—featuring just a few holes in each of the corners. These squares provide great warmth and coverage, so they're an ideal choice for a blanket.

Put It All Together

Once you master these easy granny squares for beginners, you can move on to more complex patterns. For example, this lotus bloom pattern features a textural, floral motif, and this rainbow granny square is decorated with fun, pom-pom-like accents. Or, try your hand at these cute monkey granny squares—which could be stitched together to make an adorable baby blanket.

And once you amass several granny squares, you have a ton of options for new projects to create—like a cardigan, pullover sweater, beanie, scarf, or tote bag.

No matter how simple or complex of a pattern you choose, granny squares are fun to make, a great way to use up your yarn, and a beautiful foundation for all sorts of other crochet projects.

Basic Granny Square Pattern

YOU WILL NEED

- **Size H or I crochet hook**– these are 5mm or 5.5mm in size

- **Yarn**

HOW TO CROCHET A GRANNY SQUARE

You'll need three colors of yarn for this: **Color A**= light pink, **Color B**= dark pink, and **Color C**= teal along with a 5.5mm crochet hook.

Terms used: ch= chain, dc= double crochet, sl st= slip stitch. One cluster = 3 double crochets. All terms are US Stitch Terms.

Round 1: With Color A make a slip knot. Ch 4. Join to the first ch with a sl st to make a circle/loop (or alternately make a magic loop).

Ch 2, 2dc into the loop (this forms the first cluster), ch 2, * 3dc, ch2* three times. Join with a slip stitch to the starting ch2. This completes the round and forms a square shape with 4 clusters.

Change to Color B and cut off Color A leaving a one-inch tail.

Round 2: With Color B ch2, 2dc, ch2, 3dc into the ch 2 space below

from round 1, ch1 *3dc, ch2, 3dc, ch1 into next ch2 space* three times.

Join with a slip stitch to the starting ch2. This completes the round and forms a square shape again with 8 clusters.

Change to Color C and cut off Color B leaving a one-inch tail.

Round 3: With Color C ch2, 2dc, ch1 into the ch 1 space below from round 2, ch1, (3dc, ch2, 3dc) into next ch2 space, ch1 *3dc into the ch1 space below, (3dc, ch2, 3dc) into next ch2 space below , ch1* three times

Join with a slip stitch to the starting ch2. This completes the round and forms a square shape again with 12 clusters.

Cut off Color C leaving a one-inch tail and weave in the tail.

To continue growing your Basic Granny Square infinitely: Join new color into any ch1 space below- ch2, 2dc, ch1. Then *3dc, ch1* into each of the ch1 spaces below and (3dc, ch2, 3dc, ch1) into each corner ch2 space.

BASIC GRANNY SQUARE DONE!

Once you have mastered the basic granny square pattern, you will want to make more of them!

The basic granny square is also a great kid-friendly, beginner project.

NOTES AND TIPS:

My biggest tip to you – weave those ends as you go! You do not want to end up with more than 100 granny squares with a yarn tail that needs to be tucked in.

This basic granny square pattern is for just three rounds. You can totally continue to make larger granny squares. All you need to keep in mind- the corners have two clusters with a ch2 between them.

Try making this granny square using one single color of yarn for all the rounds for a monochromatic look.

Crochet a Classic Granny Square

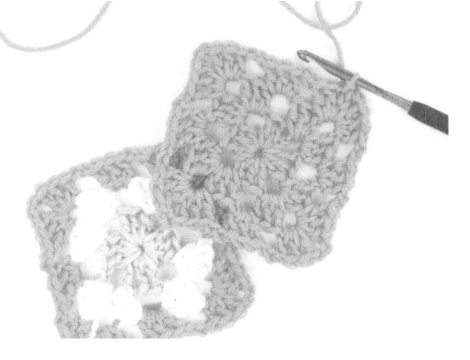

What You'll Need

Equipment / Tools

- 1 Crochet hook, size H

Materials

- 1 Skein of worsted-weight yarn

Instructions

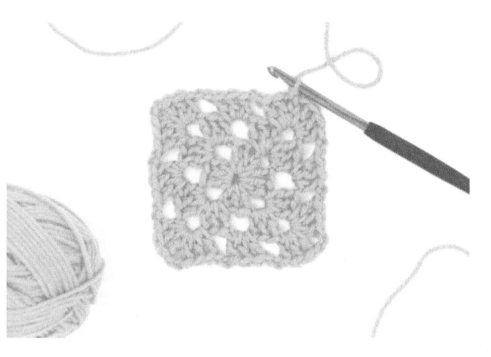

The Spruce / Mollie Johanson

A classic crochet granny square is worked in the round, using double crochet stitches worked in clusters of three with two chain stitches separating the sets.

To crochet a granny square, all you need is yarn and a crochet hook. You can use any type of yarn and any size crochet hook, although worsted weight yarn and a size H crochet hook are an easy place to start. For best results, use the crochet hook recommended for the weight of your yarn as stated on the yarn's label.

Start the Granny Square

There are different ways to start a crochet granny square, but this is the most common method and a good place to begin.

Begin with a slip knot on your crochet hook.

Next, chain 3.

Make the First Double Crochet Cluster

Groups of dc stitches are the building blocks of crochet granny squares. Each set consists of three side-by-side double crochet stitches.

The "chain 3" from the first step counts as the first double crochet stitch in the first cluster.

To complete the cluster, crochet two dc stitches into the base chain of the chain three. You should now have what looks like three dc stitches next to each other in your first group.

Next, chain 2.

Crochet the Second DC Cluster

Make another cluster of three double crochet stitches. Crochet 3 dc stitches into the base of the first chain three (the same spot where you made the other double crochet stitches from the previous grouping) round.

Chain 2.

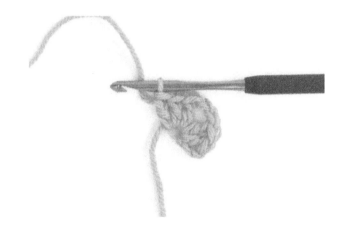

Finish Round One of the Granny Square

Repeat the previous step two more times. You should have four clusters of double crochet with a chain two space between each of them, and the last chain two hanging on the end.

To close the round and create the square shape, slip stitch into the top of the first ch 3. This ends the first round.

All those steps can sound confusing. Here's a simplified version of the first round of the granny square:

Ch 3.

2 dc in third ch from hook.

Ch 2.

3 dc in third ch from hook (same sp as before).

Ch 2.

Repeat steps 4 and 5 twice each.

Sl st to top of ch 3 to close round.

Start Round Two of the Granny Square

To start round two and all other rounds, chain 3.

As with the first round, this serves as the first double crochet of the first set.

Complete the First Double Crochet Set

Work 2 double crochet stitches right next to the chain 3 in the open corner immediately below the chain 3.

With the first dc cluster finished chain 2.

Work Around Round Two of the Granny Square

In the corner, crochet three double crochet stitches, chain 2, and crochet another 3 double crochet stitches, all in the same spot in the corner.

Chain 2.

Work every corner of the granny square this way, except for the starting corner.

Repeat for the Third Corner

Crochet around the granny square, repeating the previous step in each corner.

When you reach the corner where you started, make another cluster of 3 dc stitches, then chain 2.

Slip stitch to the top of the first chain 3 to close the round. The final corner should now look like all the others.

Round two all together:

Ch 3. 2 dc in same corner sp.

Ch 2.

Working in next corner sp: 3 dc, ch 2, 3 dc, ch 2.

Repeat step 3 twice.

3 dc in starting corner.

Ch 2.

Sl st to top of first ch 3 to close round.

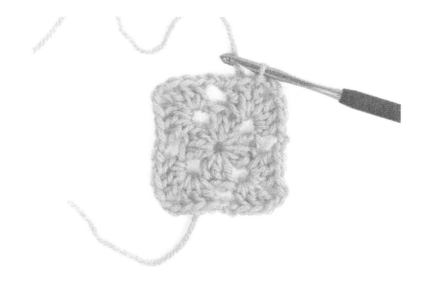

Start Round Three of the Granny Square

Begin the third round the same as the previous round.

Chain 3, then make 2 dc stitches in the same space. Chain 2.

Work Double Crochet Clusters on the Side

In this round, crochet a cluster of 3 dc stitches in the space on the side of the square, then chain 2.

Crochet Around the Third Round

Work into the corner the same way as the previous corners. Make a cluster of 3 dc stitches, chain 2, make another cluster, and chain 2.

As you work your way around the granny square, repeat the previous steps so you get a cluster on each side and two clusters in each corner.

When you reach the last corner, which was also the starting corner, make a cluster of dc stitches, chain 2, then slip stitch to close the round.

Round three all together:

Ch 3. 2 dc in same corner sp.

3 dc in next ch-2 sp. Ch 2.

Working in next corner sp: 3 dc, ch 2, 3 dc, ch 2.

Repeat steps 2 and 3 twice.

3 dc in starting corner. Ch 2.

Sl st to top of first ch 3 to close round.

Finish the Granny Square or Growing It Larger

You can finish your granny square by cutting the yarn and leaving a tail of at least six inches, then weaving in the ends.

Or you can grow the granny square larger. With each round, you will have more spaces and groups of dc along each edge. Keep adding them to grow the granny as big as you want.

Easy Crochet Granny Square by Knitcroaddict

Stitches use & code

- ch = chain
- sl st = slip stitch

- dc = double crochet

- sp = space

- REP = repeat

Instructions:

Round 1: ch 4, sl st into the 4th ch from the hook to from a ring, ch 3 (count as 1 dc), 2 dc into the ring sp, *ch 2, 3 dc into the same ring sp* REP from *TO* 2 more times, end with ch 2, sl st into the third ch that we did. Check picture below

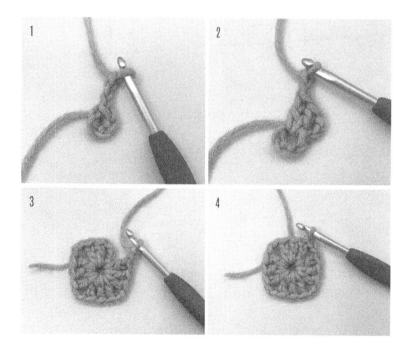

Round 2: ch 3 (count as 1 dc), 2 dc into the previous ch 2 sp, ch 1, *(3 dc, ch 2, 3 dc All into the next ch 2 sp/the corner), ch 1* REP from *TO* around and for last sp is going to be the same sp that we did the first 3 ch and 2 dc/the corner, 3 dc into that sp, ch 2, sl st into the third ch. Check picture below

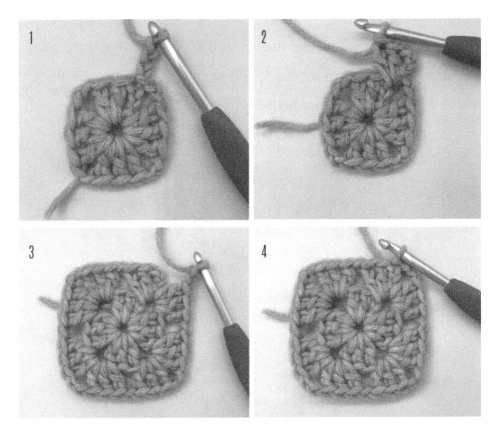

Round 3: ch 3 (count as 1 dc), 2 dc into the previous ch 2 sp, ch 1, 3

dc into the next ch 1 sp, ch 1, *(3 dc, ch 2, 3 dc All into the next ch 2 sp/the corner), ch 1, 3 dc into next ch 1 sp, ch 1* REP from *TO* around and for last sp is going to be the same sp that we did the first 3 ch and 2 dc/the corner, 3 dc into that sp, ch 2, sl st into the third ch. Check picture below

Round 4: ch 3 (count as 1 dc), 2 dc into the previous ch 2 sp, ch 1, 3

dc into the next ch 1 sp, ch 1, 3 dc into next ch 1 sp, ch 1, *(3 dc, ch 2, 3 dc All into the next ch 2 sp/the corner), ch 1, 3 dc into next ch 1 sp, ch 1, 3 dc into next ch 1 sp, ch 1* REP from *TO* around and for last sp is going to be the same sp that we did the first 3 ch and 2 dc/the corner, 3 dc into that sp, ch 2, sl st into the third ch. Check picture below

The end of round 4

Round 5 : ch 3 (count as 1 dc), 2 dc into the previous ch 2 sp, ch 1, 3 dc into the next ch 1 sp, ch 1, 3 dc into next ch 1 sp, ch 1, 3 dc into next ch 1 sp, ch 1, *(3 dc, ch 2, 3 dc All into the next ch 2 sp/the corner), ch 1, 3 dc into next ch 1 sp, ch 1, 3 dc into next ch 1 sp, ch 1, 3 dc into next ch 1 sp, ch 1* REP from *TO* around and for last sp is going to be the same sp that we did the first 3 ch and 2 dc/the corner, 3 dc into that sp, ch 2, sl st into the third ch. Check picture below

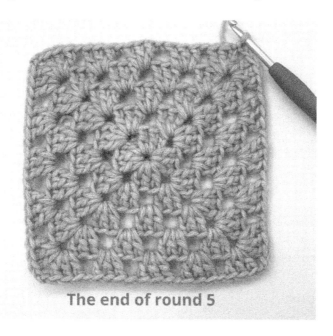

The end of round 5

From here on you're just going to repeat round 5. The only difference will be the stitch count. You will increase by 1 group of the dc before you crochet into the corner/ch 2 sp. So that means every round you will automatically increase by 4 groups of dc. Easy!

The Simple Square Pattern by Nilla K

This pattern uses US terminology

Abbreviations:

- Ch - Chain

- Dc - Double crochet

- Sk - Skip

- Sl st - Slip stitch

- St – Stitch

Pattern

Ch 5, join with sl st in the first ch to form a ring.
Round 1: Ch 3 (first dc), 2 dc in ring, *ch 3, 3 dc in ring*. Repeat from * to * two more times, ch 3. Join with sl st to ch-3.
Round 2: Join yarn in any ch-3 space. Ch 4 (first dc + ch 1), *dc in next dc, ch 1, sk 1 st, dc in next dc, ch 1, (dc, ch 3, dc) in ch-3 space, ch 1*. Repeat from * to * two more times. Dc in next dc, ch 1, sk 1 st, dc in next dc, ch 1, (dc, ch 3) in ch-3 space. Join with sl st to third ch in ch-4.

Round 3: If you use a new colour, join yarn in the first dc on any side. Ch 3 (first dc), *dc in ch-1 space, dc in dc* repeat from * to * until you reach the corner. *Make (2 dc, ch 3, 2 dc) in ch-3 space. Dc in every dc and ch-1 space until you reach corner.* Repeat from * to * two more times. Make (2 dc, ch 3, 2 dc) in ch-3 space. Join with sl st to ch-3.

Round 4: Join yarn in any ch-3 space. Ch 4 (first dc + ch 1). *Dc in next dc, ch 1, sk 1 st; repeat until you reach last dc before corner, dc in last dc, ch 1, make (dc, ch 3, dc) in ch-3 space, ch 1.* Repeat from * to * two more times. Dc in next dc, ch 1, sk 1 st; repeat until you reach last dc before corner, dc in last dc, ch 1, make (dc, ch 3) in corner. Join with sl st to third ch in ch-4.

Round 5: Repeat round 3.

Round 6: Repeat round 4.

Round 7: Repeat round 3.

Keep repeating round 4 and round 3 if you want to make a bigger square.

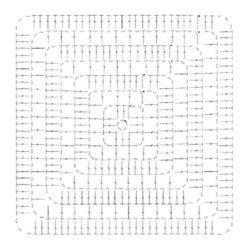

Traditional Granny Square Crochet

Stitch Guide:

- Dc cluster (double crochet cluster): 3 dc in the same st
- Dc (double crochet)
- Ch (chain)
- Sl st (slip stitch)

- Sp (space)
- Rep (repeat)

Notes:

- Ch 2 at beginning of each round counts as a dc.
- The only chain stitches are used in corner spaces. There are no chains between the clusters along each side.
- The basic pattern is: (3 dc, ch 1, 3 dc) in each ch 1 sp and 3 dc in each sp along the sides.

Basic Pattern:

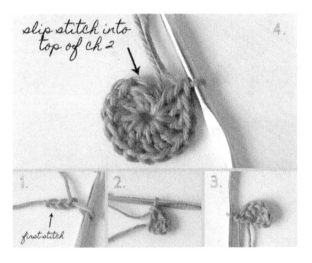

Round 1: Ch 3. 2 dc into the first ch. Ch 1, dc cluster, ch 1, dc cluster,

ch 1, dc cluster (all in the same st) Ch 1, sl st to the top of ch 2. (4 dc clusters, 4 ch 1 sp). Sl st into the next st and into ch 1 sp.

Round 2: Ch 2, 2 dc into the same sp. Ch 1, dc cluster into same sp. [Dc cluster, ch 1, dc cluster] in each ch 1 sp. Sl st to the top of ch 2. (8 dc clusters, 4 ch 1 sp). Sl st into the next st and into ch 1 sp.

Round 3: Ch 2, 2 dc into the same sp. Ch 1, dc cluster into same sp.

Dc cluster in the sp BETWEEN the 2 clusters from the previous round (as indicated below by the stitch marker). [Dc cluster, ch 1, dc cluster into the next ch 1 sp (corner sp). Dc cluster into sp between clusters from previous round] Rep [ ] **two** more times. Sl st to top of ch 2. (12 dc clusters, 4 ch 1 sp)

Sl st into the next st and into ch 1 sp.

Round 4: Ch 2, 2 dc into the same sp. Ch 1, dc cluster into same sp. Dc cluster in the sp BETWEEN the 2 clusters from the previous round, twice. [Dc cluster, ch 1, dc cluster into the next ch 1 sp. Dc cluster into sp between clusters from previous round, twice] Rep [ ] **two** more times. Sl st to top of ch 2. (16 dc clusters, 4 ch 1 sp)

Round 5: Ch 2, 2 dc into the same sp. Ch 1, dc cluster into same sp. Dc cluster in the sp BETWEEN the 2 clusters from the previous round, three times. [Dc cluster, ch 1, dc cluster into the next ch 1 sp. Dc cluster into sp between clusters from previous round, three times] Rep [ ] **two** more times. Sl st to top of ch 2. (20 dc clusters, 4 ch 1 sp)

And there you have it! That is the basic pattern for the Traditional Granny Square. You could create many different colored squares this size and sew them together to create a blanket. You could keep going row after row in this same fashion by creating one large granny square. Or you could even make yourself a colorful cardigan with your scrap yarn! The possibilities are endless!

Seriously Simple Granny Square

It's really so simple, you will be whipping these up in no time!

Simple, right? Now, let's go.

You'll need:

- Scheepjeswol Cotton 8*
- A 3mm hook.

- You can use whatever yarn you like, and the hook to match.

Gauge isn't important in this one.

First of all, chain 4 and join with a slip stitch. There are a lot of stitches into the ring, so the chain 4 foundation will have a nice tight circle anyway.

Now, for row 2 chain 2 and double crochet 11 times into the ring, joining with a slip stitch to finish with 12 stitches into your ring. This is because we want to make a square eventually, so need a total that is divisible by 4.

If you're changing colours after each row, you'll want to cut and tie off your yarn, leaving a tail to weave in.

Row 3 – chain 2, double crochet into the same stitch so you have two double crochets in one stitch and stitch two double crochets into each stitch around, leaving you with 24 stitches once you slip stitch to join. If you're not changing colours, chain 2, stitch two double crochets into the next stitch and each stitch around, with one into the last stitch, which is the same stitch that your starting chain came from.

Row 4 – here we create the square. Chain 3, two double crochet stitches into the next stitch, chain 2, and two more double crochets into the same stitch. This creates the corner. Double crochet into the next, half double crochet into the next three stitches and then double crochet into the next. Now comes the time to repeat the corner stitch (two double crochets, chain 2, two double crochets into the same stitch), then repeat the row (DC, 3xHDC, DC) until you come back round to the start. Slip stitch into the top of the chain of the first stitch.

Row 5 – Single crochet in each stitch around, with two stitches, a chain 1 and two more stitches into each corner, and you're done!

The Solid Granny Square

Materials

- Crochet hook
- Some yarn
- Tapestry needle

- Scissors

Abbreviations

- ch – chain

- ch sp – chain space

- dc- double crochet

Make a magic ring. Watch the video below if you don't know how to make a magic ring.

Round 1: Ch 3 (count as 1 dc through the entire pattern), 2 dc, ch 2, 3 dc, ch 2, 3 dc, ch 2, 3 dc, ch 2. Sl st in the top of ch 3. Pull the ring tight.

Round 2: Ch 3, 1 dc in the next 2 dc. Now work in the chain 2 sp: 2 dc, ch 2, 2 dc (first corner), *1 dc in next 3 dc. In ch sp: 2 dc, ch 2, 2 dc (second corner)*. Repeat two more times. Sl st in top of chain 3 from round 1.

Round 3: Ch 3, 1 dc in the next 4 dc. In ch 2 sp: 2 dc, ch 2, 2 dc. *1 dc in next 7 dc. In ch. sp: 2 dc, ch 2, 2 dc (corner)*. Repeat two more times. Sl st in top of chain 3 from round 2.

How to Crochet a Granny Square for Beginners

The Ultimate Granny Square

Skill Level: Easy

Gauge: 8 rows and 14 stitches = 4" in double crochet (dc)

Materials:

- Yarn of your choice
- Crochet hook of your choice
- Total yardage = 25 to 50 yards

Abbreviations:

- Slip-knot
- Chain stitch (ch)
- Slip stitch (slp st)
- Double crochet (dc)

Step 1.

Make a slip-knot

Granny squares, like all crochet projects, require making a slip-knot on your crochet hook to begin.

slip-knot

Step 2.

Make a loop.

There is more than one way to make the starting loop for a crochet granny square.

The most common method starts by chaining 4. You then make a slip-stitch (slp st) into the first chain. This creates a loop.

You can also use the magic ring, also called the magic circle, to make the starting loop. This is hands down, my favorite method.

Step 3.

Make a Cluster of Three.

Granny squares are made up of three side-by-side double crochet (dc) stitches which form a cluster.

Once you've created the starting loop, by whatever method you prefer, chain 2. This chain 2 counts as your first double crochet (dc).

Then work two more double crochets (dc) into the loop. These two double crochets, plus the chain 2, make one cluster of double crochet (dc) stitches.

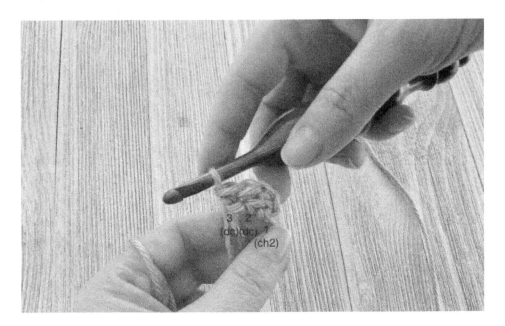

Step 4.

Chain 2.

To make the classic granny square motif, each cluster of three double crochet stitches will be followed by a chain of two. These chain twos form a space that separates each cluster and are thus commonly called a chain two space.

This will often be seen in a written pattern as "make a ch2-space".

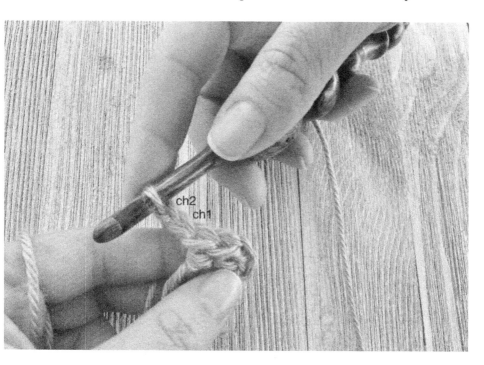

Sometimes people will chain only one after a cluster and I too, have done this.

This will make your squares slightly smaller.

So, remember, in the classic granny square method, you should always chain (ch) two after each cluster of double crochets (dc).

Step 5.

Make Another Cluster of Three.

Make another cluster by crocheting three more double crochets (dc) into the loop.

Step 6.

Repeat.

Repeat steps 4-5 two more times. When finished, you should have a total of four clusters of three double crochets and each cluster should be separated by a chain two.

These chain two spaces (ch-2 space) form the corners of the granny square. There should be four corners.

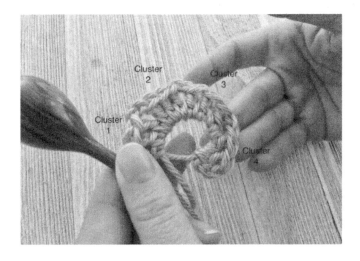

Step 7.

Close the First Round.

Regardless of the method you used to make the starting loop, you should have a hole in the center of your project at this point.

If you used the magic circle to make your starting loop then pull the tail tight to close up the center hole.

When you use the magic ring method, you can make the hole as large or as small as you would like.

To finish the round, slip stitch (slp st) into the top of the beginning chain 2 of step 4.

Granny squares can be as small or as large as you would like. The size of your crochet square is entirely up to you.

You can actually stop after the first round!

If that's what you choose, that's it, you're done. You don't even need to look at the rest of the tutorial.

However, you can also grow your granny square from this point and make it as large as you want, even large enough to cover a king-sized bed! True story.

Step 8.

Chain 5 to Begin the Second Round.

Start the second round by chaining five. The first three chains will count as the last double crochet of the very last cluster. The last two chains count as your first chain two space.

Step 9.

Form the Next Cluster.

Form your first three-double-crochet-cluster (3dc-cluster) by working three double crochets (3dc) into the chain two space (ch2-space) from the previous round. This should be the first corner of the first round.

Step 10.

Chain 2.

Chain 2 to create the corner space.

Step 11.

Form the Next Cluster.

Work 3 double crochets in the same ch2-space. Steps 9-11 create the first corner of the second round.

Step 12.

Chain 2.

Chain 2 to create the left side of the square.

Step 13.

Form the Next Cluster.

Work 3 double crochets into the next chain 2 space (the second corner of round one).

Step 14.

Chain 2.

Chain 2 to create the corner space.

Step 15.

Form the Next Cluster.

Work 3 double crochets in the same ch2-space. Steps 13-15 form the second corner of round two.

Step 16.

Repeat.

Repeat steps 12-15. This should form the bottom of the square and the third corner of the second round.

Step 17.

Chain 2.

Chain 2 to form the right side of the square.

Step 18.

Make the Next Cluster.

Work 3 double crochets in the last chain 2-space (the fourth corner of the first round).

Step 19.

Chain 2.

Chain 2 to form the corner space.

Step 20.

Make the Last Cluster.

Work two double crochets (2dc) in the last chain two space (ch2-space).

Step 21.

Close the Round.

After you've worked the 2 double crochets in the last corner, slip-stitch into the 3rd chain of the chain 5 from step 8.

The 2 double crochets plus the 3 chains of the chain 5 from step 8 create the fourth corner of the second round.

This completes round two.

Step 22.

Chain 3 to Begin Round Three.

If you want to keep growing your granny square you will start round three and any additional rounds by chaining three.

Step 23.

Form the First Cluster.

Work two double crochets into the first chain two space. This located directly to the left of the chain three created in step 22.

Step 24.

Chain 2.

Chain 2 to create the corner space.

Step 25.

Form the Corner.

Work a 3dc-cluster into the next ch2-space (the first corner of round two).

Step 26.

Chain 2.

Chain 2 to create the corner space.

Step 27.

3dc cluster in the same ch2-space.

Step 28.

Chain 2.

Chain 2 to create a new ch2-space.

Step 29.

Repeat.

Repeat steps 23-28 three more times.

Step 30.

Close the round.

Slip-stitch into the top chain of the chain 3 from step 23.

This completes the third round.

If you want to continue to grow your granny square from this point on, you essentially repeat steps 22-28 as many times as you want — with some minor changes in detail.

Step 22 says to chain 3 to start the round and this is true — IF your round starts to the RIGHT of a ch-2 space (see the 1st photo of step 23). And, then continue with step 23.

However, IF your round starts to the LEFT of ch-2 space (as in the final photo above for step 30) you will start the next round by chaining 5. This chain 5 counts as a chain 3 and a chain 2 (that will become a ch-2 space for the next round). You then work 3 dc stitches into the first ch-2 space instead of 2 dc stitches. Then carry on with steps 24-28.

Also, as your square gets larger you will notice that there will be more and dc clusters between the corners — this means that the step numbers themselves will become invalid — but the actual process of creating dc clusters and corners remains the same.

Simple Crochet Granny Square by Melanie Ham

Instructions:

Start with a magic ring

Round 1: Ch 3, DC 11 in the magic ring, finish off with slip stitch

Round 2: Ch 5, tr stitch in the same stitch the chain 5 came out of, 2 dc in each of the next 2 stitches. tr, ch 2, tr in the next stitch and then 2 dc in each of the next 2 stitches. Repeat back to beginning and sl st into the corner.

Round 3: Ch 5, tr stitch in the same stitch the chain 5 came out of, 2 dc in the next stitch and then place 1 dc in each stitch to the end of the row, but in the last stitch of the row there needs to be 2 dc. Treble (tr) stitch inside the ch 2 space of the previous round which is the corner, ch 2 and tr again in the corner. Repeat this round until desired granny square is made.

*Remember, there should be 2dc in the stitch directly before and after the corner.

Made in United States
Orlando, FL
15 April 2025

60559681R00046